The Dug Out

Amanda Whittington

SAMUELFRENCH-LONDON.CO.UK
SAMUELFRENCH.COM

FOR AMATEUR PRODUCTION ENQUIRIES

UNITED KINGDOM AND WORLD EXCLUDING NORTH AMERICA
plays@SamuelFrench-London.co.uk
020 7255 4302/01

UNITED STATES AND CANADA
info@SamuelFrench.com
1-866-598-8449

Each title is subject to availability from Samuel French,
depending upon country of performance.

The Dug Out was first performed on 30th May 2013 at the Tobacco Factory Theatre, Bristol. It was produced by Splice Theatre with the following cast:

SAMMY VAUGHAN	Ryan Calais Cameron
LEO VAUGHAN	Damson Idris
RITA LANE	Cate Cammack
CURTIS G ANTHONY	Jason Deer
GLORIA	Hamilton Lee
SASHA SIMONS	Peta Cornish
RAE BELL	Natasha Pring
HOLLY COLLINS	Annette Chown
DJ	DJ Kinsman
YOUNG CLUBBERS	Poppy Alford-Steele
	Jack Drewry
	Bella Fortune
	Dorothy Graham
	Jay Harding
	Ryan Jones
	Ashante Lake
	Martha Mondewa
	Tameka Mortimer
	Troy Orchard
	Becca Page
	Hayley Russell
	Khan Talbert Johnson
	Jake Wallace
	Jessie Wyllie
DIRECTOR/PRODUCER	Kath Rogers
CO-PRODUCER	Bob Gwilym
DESIGNER	Halla Groves-Raines
LIGHTING DESIGNER	Mike Gunning
SOUND DESIGNER	Charlie Knight
CHOREOGRAPHER	Oscar Anderson
FIGHT DIRECTOR	Kev McCurdy

The play takes place in The Dug Out, a cellar nightclub in Bristol. The set features a bar, a dancefloor, a DJ box, a payphone, banquette seating, Ladies and Gents toilet doors and one entrance/exit to a staircase and Park Row. The action takes place over one night in two time zones: December 1974 and July 1944.

CAST

In order of appearance

SAMMY VAUGHAN – (21, black), a Dug Out regular

LEO VAUGHAN – (17, black), his brother and barman

RITA LANE – (19, white), a wartime WAAF

CURTIS G ANTHONY – (21, black), an American GI

GLORIA – (21, white), an ambiguous youth

SASHA SIMONS – (17, white), a sixth form girl

RAE BELL – (17, white), her best friend

HOLLY COLLINS – (17, white), a waitress

YOUNG CLUBBERS – ensemble

A DJ plays a live set as part of the show. The suggested records are subject to rights being available.

HARLEM HOSPITALITY	Cab Calloway
MESSAGE TO YOU RUDY	Dandy Livingstone
JOHNNY TOO BAD	The Slickers
ISRAELITES	Desmond Decker
I'LL TAKE YOU THERE	The Deltones
HOTCHA-RAZZ-MA-TAZ	Cab Calloway
MR BIG STUFF	Jean Knight
NEVER CAN SAY GOODBYE	Gloria Gaynor
YOUNG GIFTED AND BLACK	Bob and Marcia
STAND BY ME	Derek Morgan
SHAME SHAME SHAME	Shirley & Company
ROOMING HOUSE BOOGIE	Cab Calloway
ANGEL OF THE MORNING	PP Arnold
PRESSURE DROP	The Maytals
REBEL MUSIC	Bob Marley
THE RETURN OF DJANGO	The Upsetters
HOUSEWIVES CHOICE	Derek and Patsy
I LEARNED ABOUT LOVE FROM HER	Cab Calloway
WHOLE WORLD'S DOWN ON ME	Ken Boothe
WHAT ABOUT YOU	Pat Rhoden
YOU WON'T LET ME GO	Buddy Johnson
KUNG FU FIGHTING	Carl Douglas

.

ACT ONE

1.

Sound of a 1940s riot on Park Street: angry shouts, bells, whistles, sirens and finally, a gunshot.

Lights up on **SAMMY**, *wearing a 1970s borstal uniform. He tunes a transistor radio. From the static comes fragments of voices, be-bop, jazz, reggae and finally,* HARLEM HOSPITALITY *by Cab Calloway.*

SAMMY *puts the radio down, glances around him, takes a notebook and pencil from his pocket, and starts to write.*

2.

HARLEM HOSPITALITY *continues. Enter* **CURTIS** *and* **RITA**, *in 1940s military uniforms.* **RITA** *has a cut to the head.*

SAMMY *looks up.*

RITA. What the hell are they doing?

CURTIS. You're safe down here, ma'am.

RITA. But they're shooting, they're actually shooting.

CURTIS. You're safe.

RITA. That coloured soldier, he's laid in the road, he needs help.

SAMMY continues to write.

CURTIS. You a nurse?

RITA. WAAF but I can't just stand by –

CURTIS. It's too late.

RITA. Let me pass.

CURTIS. Ma'am?

1

RITA. Let me pass.

CURTIS. I'm asking you very politely –

RITA. And I'm telling you, out of my way.

> CURTIS *pulls out a handkerchief and offers it to* RITA.

CURTIS. You're bleeding.

> RITA *takes the handkerchief without giving ground.*

RITA. I know why you've brought me down here.

CURTIS. Brought'cha?

RITA. So come on, if that's what you want? Come have a go and I'll kick you so hard –

CURTIS. Jeez…

RITA. I've military training.

CURTIS. We need a light.

> CURTIS *takes out a Zippo lighter and flips it open.*

RITA. I've heard what can happen if girls ain't prepared.

> CURTIS *holds up the flame.*

CURTIS. What is this place?

RITA. You tell me, you dragged me in.

CURTIS. I just saw a door, ma'am. Shoulder against it, we're out of the firing line.

RITA. Into the fire.

CURTIS. For now.

RITA. And when are you planning to free me?

CURTIS. Free you?

RITA. Will you keep me all night?

CURTIS. Ma'am, you ain't –

RITA. In this… I dunno… cellar.

CURTIS. You ain't a prisoner but I am a gentleman.

RITA. Oh?

CURTIS. If you go out, I'll have to escort'cha. And when one of them white soldiers sees us together –

RITA. We're not.

CURTIS. There's more than one war goin' on.

RITA. On Park Street?

> CURTIS *opens his cigarette case.*

CURTIS. Smoke?

RITA. Thank you, no.

CURTIS. You're shaken. You might be concussed.

> RITA *takes a cigarette.* CURTIS *lights it.*

RITA. How does it all get to this?

CURTIS. It's been comin' for weeks now. Scuffles and brawls, then Old Market on Monday: troops fighting like dogs in the street.

RITA. Why?

CURTIS. Cos a black boy went out with a white girl.

RITA. Big news.

CURTIS. It is for the white southern boys. So tonight, there's a brawl on Great George Street: white paratroopers and 545 Port Company, guys from New York who won't stand being called jigaboo.

RITA. Jigaboo?

CURTIS. Military Police round us up if we're in it or not.

RITA. And you weren't?

CURTIS. No, ma'am. They march us down Park Street. "Move, nigger," says one. One of our guys pulls a knife and all hell.

RITA. Not just a knife.

CURTIS. It's just the Military Police who got guns.

RITA. I see.

CURTIS. We're left with bottles and bricks. And I'm sorry mine hit'cha. Sincerely so, ma'am.

RITA. Well…you weren't to know.

CURTIS. You still hurting?

RITA. It's only a scratch.

CURTIS. I coulda knocked ya clean out.

RITA. Me? Not likely, I'm tough as old boots.

CURTIS. May I see?

RITA. And no brain to bash, so…

CURTIS. I don't believe that.

> RITA *take the handkerchief from her head.*

RITA. Am I free to go? Really?

CURTIS. Yes, ma'am. Although in my humble opinion, that action could prove unwise.

RITA. You Yank's got a nice way with words.

CURTIS. 1929 Quartermaster Truck Company, US Army. Private Curtis G. Anthony.

RITA. Aircraft Woman, First Class. Women's Auxilliary Air Force. Rita Lane.

CURTIS. May I have your permission to shore up the door? In case of intruders.

RITA. Private, you may.

Exit CURTIS.

Enter LEO *and the DJ.*

A prison bell rings. SAMMY *puts the notebook in his pocket and runs out, kicking over the radio as he goes. As it falls, it retunes to BBC Bristol, 1974.*

Lights snap off on SAMMY.

3.

LEO *and the DJ begin to set up the club. The 10 O'Clock News plays on the radio.*

RADIO. *Seventeen people were injured last night when two bombs exploded on a busy shopping street in Bristol. The Park Street attack is thought to be the latest in a campaign of mainland terror by the IRA. It follows bombings in Guildford, London and Birmingham in which 75 people were killed. Although no fatalities are reported, eyewitnesses describe a scene of devastation not seen in Bristol since World War Two.*

LEO. Yeh, yeh.

LEO *turns off the radio.*

(calls) Let's have some music, ey?

The DJ plays A MESSAGE TO YOU, RUDY *by Dandy Livingstone.*

LEO *directly addresses the audience (DA).*

(DA) The Dug Out, Park Row, Bristol. December, '74. Where Leo – that's me – works three nights a week on the bar. I've done everything here in my time. Collected glasses, washed glasses, poured alcoholic refreshment into glasses and

exchanged them for cash. I run the place now, more or less.
Just don't tell the boss I'm not 18 til March; and don't tell the
dole that you've seen me, all right? Cos that's how it is, innit?
That's how it has to be...

Enter **SAMMY**, *now dressed in civilian clothes and carrying a
duffel bag.*

Sammy?

SAMMY. That's me.

LEO. What you doing here?

SAMMY. Free man, aren't I?

LEO. Since when?

SAMMY. 'Bout four o'clock. Judge threw it out.

LEO. Justice prevails, man. Justice prevails!

SAMMY. Six weeks on.

LEO. S'alright, nothing's changed.

SAMMY. No?

LEO. 'Cept Park Street last night, shit...

SAMMY. Paddies in Bristol.

LEO. Boys, I t'ink we got da wrong boat.

SAMMY. It happens.

LEO. But you're back, ey. You're back!

    SAMMY *is aware of the record playing.*

SAMMY. The DJ's still a joker.

LEO. Does Mur know you're out?

SAMMY. No.

LEO. I'll phone next door, tell 'em to tell her.

SAMMY. Not yet.

LEO. Come on, you know how she is?

SAMMY. I do, yeh. I'll talk to her.

LEO. When?

SAMMY. When I'm ready, all right?

LEO. Course. Take your time. Don't rush back, not for me. Room
to myself and a record player, sweet.

SAMMY. Oi, what did I say?

LEO. 'Keep your hands off my albums'.

SAMMY. You Irish, an' all?

LEO. And I did. I just played the singles.

SAMMY. Which ones?

LEO. Only the imports. I've scratched 'em to bits.

SAMMY. Bet you have.

LEO. I looked after 'em, spacker. I looked after Mur, too. You might wanna think about that.

SAMMY. You might wanna think about getting me burn.

LEO. Get your own.

SAMMY. I'm skint.

LEO. And I'm not?

SAMMY. They sent us out with a quid. I can't sign on til Tuesday.

LEO. Nor me.

   LEO *gives* **SAMMY** *a cigarette.*

   The DJ plays JOHNNY TOO BAD.

SAMMY. Spark?

LEO. Shall I smoke it for you, an' all?

SAMMY. Stop being a girl.

   LEO *lights* **SAMMY***'s cigarette.*

LEO. And you'd know about girls, ey?

SAMMY. I know more than you.

LEO. That's what you think.

SAMMY. Oh, yeh?

LEO. Six weeks… it's a long time, innit?

SAMMY. Not long enough for you to get lucky.

LEO. Well, perhaps some things have changed… for you.

SAMMY. Like what?

LEO. Girls get bored easy, don't they? Bored of hanging around. They go off.

SAMMY. Who with?

LEO. Some University student or Lord.

SAMMY. Lord?

LEO. Posh girls, that's what they want in the end.

SAMMY. She's only from Clifton. She's rich but she's not like… you mick.

LEO. You're the mick if you think she'll be waiting.

SAMMY. I don't.

LEO. So how come you're straight here?

SAMMY. I wanted a drink.

LEO. You're the big mick. Getting picked up for... what?

SAMMY. Pint of Lamot.

LEO. What, Sam?

Beat.

SAMMY. Wrong place, wrong time.

LEO. Doing what?

SAMMY. Nothing.

LEO. You got banged up for nothing?

SAMMY. You know what it's like out there... yeh.

LEO *pours* **SAMMY** *a pint.*

LEO. On the house. Don't tell the boss.

SAMMY. Like I would.

LEO. And let's drink to freedom.

SAMMY. Let's drink.

LEO. She's been down, as it happens. Asking about where you was.

SAMMY. And you told her...?

LEO. I wasn't your keeper. Zoo-keeper.

SAMMY. Piss off.

LEO. But it's all done now, innit?

SAMMY. You reckon?

LEO. It is. You're out. No problems 'cept bombs in the street.

SAMMY. They can blow the whole town up for me.

The DJ plays THE ISRAELITES *by Desmond Decker.*

LEO. But not til tomorrow, ey, Sam?

The YOUNG CLUBBERS *flood in. The club night begins and the* YOUNG CLUBBERS *dance to* THE ISRAELITES.

4.

As the song plays, **GLORIA** *enters the club. His style is mid-70s Bowie with shades of 40's Hollywood.*

GLORIA. Is it a bird, is it a plane?

LEO. *(TA)* Is the circus in town?

    The **YOUNG CLUBBERS** *stare at* **GLORIA.**

GLORIA. What are you looking at?

LEO. *(TA)* Still, things like him-or-her don't bother me. Live an' let live, an' all that. Just so long as they don't come too close, if you know what I mean?

    SAMMY *is propping up the bar.*

GLORIA. Hello, stranger.

LEO. *(TA)* So long as they know that it's Ladies and Gents here. We don't have no door in between.

GLORIA. Well, it's been terribly dull here without you. No smouldering tension, no withering looks.

SAMMY. Leo?

    SAMMY *pushes his empty glass to* **LEO.**

GLORIA. Still, I'm sure you'll have wonderful stories to share. All lads together, a Boy's Own adventure.

SAMMY. Who told you?

GLORIA. My sources are never revealed.

SAMMY. *(gesturing to* **LEO***)* That div?

GLORIA. He's the soul of discretion.

LEO. The Soul of Discretion Man.

SAMMY. Who?

LEO. People talk, Sam.

SAMMY. Too much. You got draw?

LEO. No.

SAMMY. Yes, you have.

LEO. You want the shirt off my back, now?

SAMMY. No way, it's crap.

LEO. Crap? It's *Man at C&A*, this. Four quid.

SAMMY. You wuz robbed.

GLORIA. Well you'd know. Welcome home.

GLORIA *offers a small bag of cannabis to* SAMMY.

SAMMY. I don't want it from you.

GLORIA. That's what they all say.

SAMMY. Sod off.

GLORIA. Suit yourself.

GLORIA *puts the bag into* SAMMY*'s pocket.*

SAMMY. I'm signing on, Tuesday. I'll sort you out then.

GLORIA. Nice lunch at a Bernie Inn?

SAMMY. Shut it.

SAMMY *moves into a corner to roll a spliff.*

GLORIA. Prawn cocktail to start?

LEO *gives a pound note to* GLORIA.

LEO. Best he owes me.

GLORIA. Little bro' bails him out yet again.

LEO. How do you know where he's been?

GLORIA. Angry young man goes AWOL? It's that or he's run off to sea.

LEO. No chance of that, he can't swim.

GLORIA. So what was he in for?

LEO. Search me.

GLORIA. Shall I?

LEO. And just watch your step with our Sammy, right? Don't wind him up.

GLORIA. But he's my best clockwork soldier.

LEO. Word to the wise, as Mur says. Let him be.

GLORIA. Let him be what?

LEO. Not tonight, Josephine.

GLORIA. Gloria.

LEO. Not tonight.

The DJ plays I'LL TAKE YOU THERE *by The Deltones.*

5.

Enter **SASHA**, **RAE** *and* **HOLLY**. **SASHA** *dresses as an urban gypsy.* **RAE**, *in jeans, carries a camera.* **HOLLY** *wears hotpants.*

LEO. *(DA)* It weren't always like this, me and him. I could make Sammy laugh just like that. *(clicks his fingers)* He once laughed so much, his dinner came out of his nose. I'm still pretty funny I reckon, but who knows what's happened to him?

LEO *catches sight of the girls.*

(DA) Well, Sasha happened. But wouldn't she put a smile on your face?

SASHA. It's just like a war zone out there.

RAE. It is a war zone.

SASHA. What on earth do they think they'll achieve?

RAE. A free Ireland.

HOLLY. But why bomb us to get it?

RAE. We're an occupying force.

HOLLY. Excuse me? No one from Bristol's gone out with a gun.

RAE. Except the Glosters.

HOLLY. Well, no one from Wimpy has. What did we do?

SASHA. Nothing. It must have been awful.

HOLLY. Sash, it was worse than *The Exorcist.*

RAE. Sash?

SASHA. You've seen *The Exorcist?*

HOLLY. Three times.

SASHA. Wow.

HOLLY. And it's kids stuff compared to last night. Shop windows blown out in front of your eyes, glass flying everywhere, plastic dead bodies all over.

RAE. Plastic?

SASHA. Showroom dummies, she means.

HOLLY. Laid out in the street, eyes wide open.

SASHA. So Dada.

HOLLY. So what?

RAE. Dada. It's an artistic movement.

SASHA. Abstract, surrealist, you know? Like the torn decorations in Rayner's shop window. That Dylan cover 'blowing in the wind'.

HOLLY. And the strip club in full view of everyone.

RAE. Yes, it's appalling. Those costumes hung up there like shackles.

SASHA. I know. We should picket or something.

RAE. Expose them.

HOLLY. They're already exposed, luv. Full frontal.

RAE. Photo-journalistically, luv.

HOLLY. In't that sick?

RAE. Sick?

HOLLY. There's real people's blood on the street, would you snap that, an' all?

SASHA. She doesn't actually snap –

RAE. I've the right to respond as an artist. And it isn't like anyone died.

HOLLY. They could have. I could have. Wimpy was packed.

SASHA. Are you still in shock, do you think?

HOLLY. Oh, definitely, yeh.

SASHA. Well, if you feel shaky, just say. If you get any flashbacks or –

RAE. Oh God!

SASHA. What?

RAE. Sammy's back.

SASHA. Where? Has he seen me?

RAE. Oh, definitely.

SASHA. Don't look!

    LEO *is collecting glasses.*

LEO. Ladies…

RAE. Women.

LEO. And who's the new girl? Woman.

SASHA. Holly Collins.

LEO. She at Colston with you?

SASHA. No, no. She works in Wimpy.

LEO. *(to* **HOLLY***)* All right, my lover?

SASHA. And she's never been before, have you?

HOLLY. Is this it? The best club in Bristol?

LEO. Yep, this is *The Dug Out* and I'm Leo Vaughan. I virtually run the place –

HOLLY. I'm stuck to the carpet.

SASHA. It's only beer.

HOLLY. It's filthy.

RAE. It's underground.

HOLLY. What sort of music is that?

LEO. *I'll Take You There.* The Deltones. And I can, just say the word.

HOLLY. Don't they play disco?

RAE. Oh yes, and The Osmonds?

LEO. He might for me. Any requests?

HOLLY. *Shame, Shame, Shame.* Shirley & Co.

RAE. Puke.

SASHA. Rae? Three barley wines.

HOLLY. That's a tramp's drink. Barcardi and Coke.

RAE. We can't afford –

LEO. Girls… women… whatever… they're on the house. Don't tell the boss.

> **LEO** *goes to have a word with the DJ.*

HOLLY. Is he backward or something?

SASHA. That's Sammy's brother.

HOLLY. What, as in "soul brother?"

RAE. No, as in "sibling".

HOLLY. Fancy him, do you?

RAE. Me? No, not at all, what a crass question.

HOLLY. If you say so. Where's the Ladies?

RAE. The toilets.

SASHA. Far corner.

HOLLY. You coming?

SASHA. Well, yes, if you want me to… Rae?

RAE. We're feminists, Sasha. We don't pee in pairs.

> **HOLLY** *crosses the dancefloor.*

SASHA. But we pee, all the same. At the same time, sometimes.

> **HOLLY** *gets a wolf-whistle from a* **YOUNG CLUBBER.**

RAE. Philistines.

> **RAE** *goes to the bar and* **SASHA** *follows* **HOLLY** *to the Ladies, watched by* **SAMMY**.

LEO. *(TA)* Holly Collins…

6.

> *As* **SAMMY** *comes out of his corner as if to follow* **SASHA**. *The music cross-fades to* HOTCHA RAZZ MA TAZZ *by Cab Calloway.* **CURTIS** *returns.* **SAMMY** *turns to watch him.*

RITA. What's happening? Are you all right?

CURTIS. I went to the door, shot the bolt.

RITA. Shot it, you don't have a gun.

CURTIS. Closed it tight. Put a old crate up, came down the steps and…

> **CURTIS** *holds up a handful of candles.*

RITA. Candles!

CURTIS. Let there be light.

> **CURTIS** *and* **RITA** *place the candles.*

RITA. Should we be doing this? You know, with the blackout?

CURTIS. We're way underground. And we can't sit all night in the dark.

RITA. All night?

CURTIS. Could be. The men ain't going nowhere, there's barricades.

RITA. Why can't they just march 'em back?

CURTIS. Ma'am, we ain't taking orders tonight.

> **CURTIS** *and* **RITA** *light the candles.*

RITA. Will we ever have peace, do you think?

CURTIS. In Europe? I guess.

RITA. And street lights again?

CURTIS. I dream of street lights. And nectarines fresh from the tree.

RITA. Nectarines?

CURTIS. The taste of home. Knoxville, Tennessee.

RITA. My father grows carrots. We put 'em in jam now. Needs must.

CURTIS. Carrot jam. Still sounds like heaven to me.

RITA. Food not so good on the base?

CURTIS. You wouldn't give it to a dog.

RITA. I thought an Army marched on its stomach?

CURTIS. Not when you're serving Jim Crow.

RITA. Your President's Roosevelt.

CURTIS. Sure. But he ain't doing jack for our boys.

RITA. Jim Crow?

CURTIS. Black units, black quarters, black pass-outs.

RITA. What do you mean?

CURTIS. Long story.

RITA. And we've a long night ahead.

> **SAMMY** *retreats to his corner, leading the cross-fade to* MR BIG STUFF *by Jean Knight.*

7.

> **RAE** *is rolling a cigarette.* **LEO** *brings her a tray of drinks.*

LEO. *(TA)* Rae rolls her own. She takes care of herself, so she tells me, except she don't leave Sasha's side. They're going to London next year. Art school. They'll be drinking champagne there, I suppose? But for now, it's two barley wines...
(to **RAE***)...* and a Barcardi & Coke.

> **RAE** *offers* **LEO** *a pound note.*

RAE. Thank you.

LEO. S'right, it's sorted.

RAE. For Holly? A down-payment for services rendered, I'm sure.

LEO. 'Ey?

RAE. Take for two barley wines. Women like us won't be bought.

> **RAE** *shoves the money into* **LEO** *'s hand.*

LEO. Do they want change, though?

RAE. Well, yes.

LEO. I won't bring it over. Don't want to belittle you, ey?

> **LEO** *returns to the bar.*

RAE. Bollocks!

    HOLLY *and* **SASHA** *come out of the Ladies.*

SASHA. Is he still out there?

HOLLY. Still in the corner.

SASHA. Skulking.

HOLLY. So he should be.

SASHA. Look at him. Well, don't. But look at him sat there pretending he's not.

HOLLY. It's funny. I thought he'd be handsome.

SASHA. He is. Well, he was.

HOLLY. Til you saw him for what he was.

SASHA. Yes.

HOLLY. A user.

    Beat.

SASHA. Yes.

    HOLLY *and* **SASHA** *cross to* **RAE.**

HOLLY. You've got to forget him now, Sasha.

SASHA. I have.

HOLLY. Boys ain't worth it, I've told you.

SASHA. I know.

HOLLY. Today's the First Day of the Rest of Your Life. With your mates, right?

SASHA. My sisters, yes.

    HOLLY *sees* **RAE** *rolling a cigarette.*

HOLLY. What are you doing?

RAE. Synchronized swimming.

HOLLY. Rollies?

RAE. It's an act of creation.

HOLLY. Oh, I must tell my Granddad.

SASHA. Rae, move up, let Holly sit down.

RAE. Of course. Take the weight off your subordinate footwear.

HOLLY. I thought we'd come here to dance?

SASHA. We have.

HOLLY. Well, let's get out there. Let's show him you're over him.

SASHA. I will, don't worry. When the right record comes on.

HOLLY. They're all dire, what's the difference?

RAE. Excuse me!

> **GLORIA** *sashays across the club, passing* **HOLLY***.*

GLORIA. *(to* **HOLLY***)* Mmmm, Marilyn.

HOLLY. *(to* **SASHA***)* Gloria?

SASHA. Told you.

RAE. And yes, he's a gay. Got a problem with that?

SASHA. She. That's what they want to be called.

> **HOLLY** *watches* **GLORIA** *disappear into the Ladies.*

HOLLY. Ziggy Stardust…

SASHA. When they wear make-up like that?

RAE. I'm sure. But as Germaine Greer says, if we accept 'her' gender definition, what she's actually aspiring to is the Stereotype –

HOLLY. *(to* **RAE***)* Thank you, Bamber Gascoigne. *(to* **SASHA***)* When you're quite ready, I'm waiting.

> **HOLLY** *takes her drink and stands by the Ladies.*

> *The DJ plays* NEVER CAN SAY GOODBYE.

RAE. Run along.

SASHA. Do you have to go on about all that tonight?

RAE. All what?

SASHA. *The Female Eunuch.* There's more than one book in the world.

RAE. Oh, so now I'm being censored?

SASHA. Let's just make Holly feel welcome, shall we?

RAE. You'll be wearing her Wonderbra next.

SASHA. She's not what you think.

RAE. She's a waitress at Wimpy.

SASHA. God, you're a snob.

RAE. No, I'm a vegan, like you.

SASHA. I was.

RAE. Sasha!

SASHA. Diets are an expression of patriarchy. And most of the time, I was famished.

RAE. What does your Mum say to that?

SASHA. It's my life, I'll cook for myself.

RAE. And for Holly, I suppose?

SASHA. Well, you can't eat nut roast all your life.

Beat.

RAE. You've changed since you met her.

SASHA. I change every day. It's called growing up, Rae.

RAE. It's like I don't know who you are any more.

SASHA. And who's fault is that?

RAE. Not mine.

SASHA. It never is.

RAE. What do you mean?

SASHA. You push people away.

RAE. No, I don't.

SASHA. Yes, you do. Look at Leo. He just tries to make conversation and…

RAE. Leo's a man.

SASHA. So?

RAE. So I'm out with my sister.

SASHA. Holly's a sister.

RAE. Barbie's sister.

SASHA. Look, she's a lesbian, Rae.

Beat.

RAE. A what?

SASHA. A lesbian. Women who like –

RAE. Yes, I know what they are. She can't be.

SASHA. And don't you dare tell.

RAE. She's a teenager. Lesbians… aren't.

SASHA. They're not all like Miss. Maddox, you know?

RAE. She wears make-up.

SASHA. Rae, you're so blinkered sometimes.

RAE. Why am I? You've only just met her. How come you know what she is?

SASHA. Cos she told me.

RAE. In Wimpy?

SASHA. No… later.

RAE. She actually said it out loud?

SASHA. Yes. Sort of. She told me she doesn't like boys.

RAE. Well, we don't, politically speaking.

SASHA. She said she's had sex with five of them –

RAE. Five?

SASHA. But she's never felt anything... you know...

RAE. She's making it up.

SASHA. No, she isn't. We've spoken in depth.

RAE. What about?

SASHA. All sorts of... oh, God...

RAE. What?

SASHA. Sammy's coming over, don't look.

> **SASHA** *turns away as* **SAMMY** *goes upstairs, barely glancing at her as he passes.*

RAE. He's going out for a smoke.

> **SASHA** *watches* **SAMMY** *leaving.*

SASHA. Are you sure?

RAE. He'll be back.

> *Beat.*

SASHA. I don't want him back. Six weeks without a word.

RAE. Barley wine?

SASHA. Bastard.

RAE. They are.

> *The DJ plays* YOUNG, GIFTED AND BLACK *by Bob & Marcia.*

> **GLORIA** *comes out of the Ladies where* **HOLLY** *is waiting.*

GLORIA. They're playing my song. Well, two-thirds of it.

HOLLY. Mine too.

> **GLORIA** *gives* **HOLLY** *the once-over.*

GLORIA. Oh? How young, exactly?

HOLLY. How gifted?

GLORIA. You'll see.

> **GLORIA** *takes* **HOLLY** *to dance, watched by* **SAMMY**. *The* **YOUNG CLUBBERS** *dance too.* YOUNG, GIFTED AND BLACK *plays through, then cross-fades to* STAND BY ME *by Derrick Morgan.*

8.

SAMMY *watches* CURTIS *and* RITA. STAND BY ME *plays at low volume.*

CURTIS. You've seen in the pubs: Black Tuesday/White Wednesday? The British ain't put them signs up.

RITA. Jim Crow…

CURTIS. There's two US Armies and two kinds of soldier. The white boys are trained up to fight. The black boys are storemen and drivers and cooks; and tonight, the 545… well, they won't take it no more. Last Friday, they would not come out for reveille.

RITA. Reveille?

CURTIS. The morning bugle call. Song rang true that day, I tell ya.

RITA. What song's that?

CURTIS. *(sings)* "I can't get em up/ Can't get em up/ Can't get em up this morning/ I can't get em up/Can't get em up/Can't get em up at all".

RITA. Nice!

CURTIS. *(sings)* "Corporals worse than the private/Sergeant's worse than the corporal/Lieutenants worse than the sergeant/And the captain's worst of all'.

RITA. We don't have nothing like reveille. Not at Pucklechurch.

CURTIS. Pucklechurch?

RITA. That's where I'm based. Eight miles or so out of town.

CURTIS. You're a regular?

RITA. Two years now. Volunteered.

CURTIS. Me too. I read there's a new law: "Discrimination Prohibited in the Selection and Training of Men Based on Race or Colour". Quit my job and signed up.

RITA. What job was that, then?

CURTIS. Bricklayer, ma'am. But I do have a college education.

RITA. I'm as thick as a plank.

CURTIS. Major and minor in Mathematics and Chemistry.

RITA. Crikey.

CURTIS. I'm proficient in algebra, plane geometry, analytical geometry and supherical trigonometry. I also learned Spanish and Portuguese.

RITA. Say a bit.

CURTIS. *Un poco.*

RITA. What's that?

CURTIS. A bit.

RITA. Say something proper.

CURTIS. *Dígame, cual es la mejor manera de cocinar zanahorias.*

RITA. That sounds lovely. What does it mean?

CURTIS. Tell me, what's the best way to cook carrots?

RITA. *(laughing)* No!

CURTIS. I swear. *Dígame…*

RITA. *Dígame…*

CURTIS. *Cual es la mejor manera…*

RITA. *Cual es la mejor manera.*

CURTIS. *De cocinar zanahorias.*

RITA. *De cocinar zanahorias.*

CURTIS. And what would your Pa say to that?

RITA. Blimey, girl!

CURTIS. *Joder, niña!*

RITA. You talk like a poet, you do.

CURTIS. *Tú también.* You too.

> **SAMMY** *laughs and exits, with spliff.*

9.

> **GLORIA** *and* **HOLLY** *dance to the bar, laughing.* **RAE** *returns to* **SASHA** *with drinks.* **LEO** *addresses the audience.*

LEO. *(DA)* A question for you: what's the difference between a barman and a bog seat? Answer? A bog seat only deals with one arse at a time. But I'm good at my job and there's benefits, too. Sleeping in, that's one of 'em. Chatting up girls, a requirement I'm able to meet. And put any old bloke on that side of the bar and he's 50 per cent more good-looking, straight off. So it's a good job for me, for now. Til my actual life starts. And it will, soon enough. Soon enough…

RAE. "Cheeseburger, chips and my sexual preference."

SASHA. I'm sorry?

RAE. Is that how it was?

SASHA. Can we please change the subject?

RAE. Is that how she admitted it?

SASHA. All right, for the last time: I went into Wimpy one afternoon, Holly was there. It was quiet, we started to chat, I went back.

RAE. Secretly?

SASHA. Yes, as a matter of fact. As a vegan. And I liked her –

RAE. As well as the burgers.

SASHA. She's different, she's funny, she's honest, she's new. She's someone who'll liven things up.

RAE. Unlike me.

SASHA. I didn't say that. I just thought that when Sammy finally came back…

RAE. What?

SASHA. I wanted to show him that things had moved on. That my life was better than his. More fun, more exciting, more glamorous.

RAE. Without him and me.

SASHA. Read my lips, Rae. You're Still My Best Friend.

RAE. So you say.

SASHA. But we're seventeen now – and we don't own each other, do we?

Beat.

RAE. Are we still going to art college?

SASHA. Yes. If we pass our exams, get a place.

RAE. And I can still come to the house? You know, when my Mum gets…

SASHA. Of course.

RAE. I can still be a part of the family?

SASHA. For God's sake, you *are* part of the family. You're closer to Mum than I am. You can talk to her. I can't, can I?

Beat.

RAE. Sasha? Are you trying to tell me you're a lez?

SASHA. Oh, for God's sake!

RAE. Is that why you and Sammy –

SASHA. Rae, you can like homosexuals without 'liking' them.

RAE. And we can lie to ourselves.

SASHA. I'm a liberated woman. And as such, I accept, include and embrace. But not in the physical sense.

RAE. But if you did – if you are – I'd be totally, totally cool with it.

SASHA. Know what, I wish sometimes I was. At least I'd be out of this...

RAE. What?

Beat.

SASHA. With Sammy, that's all.

RAE. Do you want me to talk to him? Try to find out where he's been, what he's –

SASHA. No! I just want to... oh, I don't know, I don't know, I don't know...

RAE. It's all right. I'll come back tonight.

SASHA. I think perhaps I should be on my own.

RAE. I've got draw.

> **SASHA** *looks at* **RAE**.

SASHA. Why don't you smoke it with Leo?

RAE. No, thank you.

SASHA. Oh, come on, you've liked him forever. And he likes you.

RAE. As if?

SASHA. Rae, it's obvious.

RAE. Is it? You saw him ogling her.

SASHA. And where will that get him? She's not going to stand in your way.

> **RAE** *looks over at* **HOLLY** *and* **GLORIA**, *laughing together.*

RAE. Look at her, lost in confusion. Oppressing herself.

SASHA. Is she?

RAE. Open your eyes. She won't meet a lesbian looking like that.

SASHA. Long hair and fingernails.

RAE. She's got a lot to learn, Sasha.

SASHA. I know. It's terribly sad.

> **HOLLY** *and* **GLORIA** *burst into peals of laughter.*

RAE. Leo...

SASHA. He's likes you, trust me.

RAE. He's done nothing about it.

SASHA. Rae, you're a radical feminist. Do it yourself.

    Beat.

RAE. How?

    Music cross-fades to SHAME, SHAME, SHAME *by Shirley and Company.*

10.

    LEO *is behind the bar, serving* **HOLLY** *and* **GLORIA.**

LEO. For the lady and…

GLORIA. The tramp.

HOLLY. Shame, Shame, Shame!

LEO. See, I got it for you.

HOLLY. Thanks, Louis.

LEO. Leo.

HOLLY. Gemini.

LEO. Nice name.

GLORIA. I think perhaps she's being ironic.

HOLLY. Am I?

LEO. Not as ironic as me.

    RAE *is pushed over by* **SASHA**.

RAE. Two barley wines.

LEO. "We can rebuild him."

SASHA. Please?

HOLLY. Come on, let's dance.

    LEO *dances in Steve Austen-style slow motion.*

LEO. "We have the technology. We have the capability to build the world's first Ironic Man."

GLORIA. With a six million dollar smile.

LEO. All right, Gaylord.

RAE. That's a pejorative –

HOLLY. Look! He'd blush if he weren't black. *(to* **LEO***)* You don't mind me calling you that?

LEO. S'what I am.

HOLLY. I know you're supposed to say coloured but that just sounds stupid to me.

GLORIA. I'm multi-coloured: turquoise, yellow, pejorative pink.

LEO. I've got a yellow car.

GLORIA. Oh, like Noddy?

LEO. It's on bricks at the moment in Mur's back yard but I'm training myself in mechanics.

> **HOLLY** *is dancing on her own.*

SASHA. That's interesting, isn't it, Rae?

LEO. I've already learned spark plugs and cleaned out the carb –

RAE. Good.

GLORIA. She likes greasy things.

LEO. Does she?

> **LEO** *looks at* **RAE,** *who hesitates.*

RAE. My change?

LEO. Yeh, yeh… your change.

> **LEO** *hands* **RAE** *her change.*

SASHA. And?

RAE. And excuse me?

LEO. It's right. I counted it twice.

RAE. The thing is you probably don't care but I'm doing a project.

LEO. A project?

> **RAE** *holds up her camera.*

RAE. It's Andy Warholesque.

HOLLY. Whatever that is.

RAE. A microcosmic view of the counter-culture with a focus on gender and race:

SASHA. Part Pop-Art, part photo-journo.

RAE. With a Marxist agenda, of course.

LEO. Course.

HOLLY. That's clear as mud, then.

GLORIA. Miaow…

RAE. And I wondered… can I take your photo.

HOLLY. Sasha! Come on.

SASHA. But Sammy's not here.

HOLLY. No. I am.

> HOLLY *pulls* SASHA *onto the dancefloor without a glance to* LEO.

LEO. She's ain't interested, is she?

GLORIA. In a word, no.

LEO. Story of my life.

GLORIA. Yes but sombeody might be?

LEO. Who's that, then?

> GLORIA *nods to* RAE.

RAE. Artistically, anyway.

> LEO *looks at* RAE *and strikes a Bionic Man pose.*

LEO. "Leo Vaughan will be that man. Better than he was before. Better – faster – stronger."

> LEO *heads off in slow-motion.*

RAE. Is he taking the piss out of me?

GLORIA. Yes. Run along.

> RAE *follows* LEO *with her camera.*

> *The* YOUNG CLUBBERS *dance to* SHAME SHAME SHAME.

> *The track plays through, then cross-fades to* ROOMING HOUSE BOOGIE *by Cab Calloway.*

> *As it cross-fades,* SAMMY *enters the club, his vision now a little blurred.*

11.

> SAMMY *watches* CURTIS *watching* RITA, *who holds her hand to a candle for a trace of warmth.*

CURTIS. You cold?

RITA. A little.

CURTIS. Have this.

> CURTIS *takes off his jacket.*

RITA. I couldn't.

CURTIS. You can.

RITA. No, really, I'm…

CURTIS. Sure.

> **CURTIS** *puts his jacket down.*

RITA. I should do a few star-jumps or something.

CURTIS. You learn that too in the WAAF?

RITA. We got put through our paces in training. Gymnastics, all sorts.

CURTIS. I got a better idea.

> **CURTIS** *does a jive step.*

RITA. What's that?

CURTIS. You don't jive?

RITA. Not at Pucklechurch.

CURTIS. But you know of the soft-shoe shuffle?

RITA. I've heard of it. Never seen it done by an expert, though.

CURTIS. Ah, it's easy when you know how.

RITA. For you, perhaps?

CURTIS. Try it.

RITA. I couldn't.

CURTIS. Who says?

RITA. I can waltz and foxtrot but nothing like that.

> **CURTIS** *leads* **RITA** *into the dance.*

CURTIS. No? One-two, one-two, one-two.

RITA. Oh, my!

CURTIS. You're good.

RITA. Am I?

CURTIS. For a white girl, you're good!

> **CURTIS** *and* **RITA** *lead the* **YOUNG CLUBBERS** *as they dance 40s-style to* ***ROOMING HOUSE BOOGIE***. *The steps subliminally pass across the dancefloor, like Chinese Whispers.*

12.

> **SAMMY** *goes onto the dancefloor, moving into the* ***ROOMING HOUSE BOOGIE*** *dance.* **HOLLY** *and* **SASHA** *are dancing flirtatiously.*

SASHA. He's here. He's watching.

HOLLY. Who cares?

> **GLORIA** *passes* **SAMMY**.

GLORIA. Stoned?

SAMMY. Just mellowing out.

GLORIA. And enjoying the floor show, I see.

> **HOLLY** *raises the temperature of the 40s-style dance.*

> **SAMMY** *shouts above the music to* **SASHA**.

SAMMY. What are you doing?

SASHA. I'm sorry?

SAMMY. Dancing like that.

SASHA. Do I know you?

HOLLY. Sasha?

> **HOLLY** *tries to dance* **SASHA** *away but* **SAMMY** *pulls her back.*

SAMMY. Dance with me.

SASHA. Have we met?

SAMMY. Stop messing about.

SASHA. Me?

HOLLY. Leave her alone, please?

SAMMY. Who's she?

HOLLY. Holly Collins, her best friend.

SASHA. Joint best friend.

HOLLY. And she's with me tonight, all right?

SASHA. Holly?

HOLLY. Sisters, aren't we?

SAMMY. More like witches.

SASHA. Well, better a witch than a wanker.

> **SASHA** *pushes past* **SAMMY** *and goes into the Ladies.*

> *Music cross-fades to* ANGEL OF THE MORNING *by Pp Arnold.*

> **HOLLY** *is now dancing towards* **SAMMY**.

HOLLY. All right?

SAMMY. What do you think?

HOLLY. Wanna dance?

SAMMY *gestures to the Ladies.*

SAMMY. Go get her.

HOLLY. I don't think that's wise.

SAMMY. I wanna talk to her.

HOLLY. Talk to me.

SAMMY. Why should I?

HOLLY. Cos I know.

HOLLY *pulls* SAMMY *into the dance.*

SAMMY. Know what?

HOLLY. We've got very close since you cleared off.

SAMMY. I didn't.

HOLLY. Well, she thinks you did.

SAMMY. What's she said?

HOLLY. Oh… just that you're a shit.

SAMMY. She knew that from the start.

HOLLY. No word for six weeks. Not even a phonecall.

SAMMY. I tried.

HOLLY. When?

SAMMY. Loads of times.

HOLLY. Except when you said you would. Poor girl, she's been sat by the phone.

SAMMY. I ran out of coins, didn't I?

HOLLY. It's two-bloody-pence in a box.

SAMMY. If you find one that isn't smashed up.

HOLLY. There's one up there. Oh, except you haven't been in.

SAMMY. Look, I did try to phone her, all right?

HOLLY. What's her number?

SAMMY. You what?

HOLLY. Her telephone number, what is it?

SAMMY. 265913.

HOLLY. No.

SAMMY. 265139.

HOLLY. 265931.

SAMMY. And you'd know?

HOLLY. Like I told you, we're close. And Sammy? We could be, an' all.

SAMMY. You reckon?

HOLLY. Oh, let's not play games. I saw you looking at me.

SAMMY. I was looking at her.

HOLLY. Course you were.

> **HOLLY** *moves closer to* **SAMMY**.

SAMMY. What's going on?

HOLLY. Me and you, if you like? Up on the Downs, where you took her. Tonight.

SAMMY. It's December.

HOLLY. I'll keep you warm.

> **HOLLY** *leans into* **SAMMY** *until he can't help but touch her.*

SAMMY. Tonight?

HOLLY. In your dreams, dickhead.

> **HOLLY** *pushes* **SAMMY** *away and goes back to the bar.*

CURTIS. Ma'am, you're the best dance partner I –

> **SAMMY** *roars in frustration and kicks a table.* **CURTIS** *and* **RITA** *stop dancing.*

RITA. Curtis…

CURTIS. Stay here.

RITA. Don't go, it might be the Military –

CURTIS. Stay.

> *Exit* **CURTIS**. **SAMMY** *goes angrily into the Gents.*

13.

> **RAE** *is following* **LEO** *with her camera.*

LEO. Got a good 'un yet, have you?

RAE. I might if you stop showing off.

LEO. Let me take one of you.

RAE. I'm the auteur.

> **LEO** *takes the camera.*

LEO. Say cheese.

RAE. They're not that sort of picture.

LEO. They are now.

LEO *photographs* **RAE**.

RAE. You're wasting the film.

LEO. Why? You've got a nice enough smile.

RAE. "Nice".

LEO. You have.

> **LEO** *offers* **RAE** *the camera back but* **GLORIA** *intervenes, taking it from him.*

GLORIA. May I?

> ANGEL OF THE MORNING *cross-fades To* PRESSURE DROP *by The Maytals.*

LEO. You've got a smile and I've got a car.

RAE. You can drive?

LEO. Course I can. I've just not passed my test yet, that's all.

RAE. It's some kind of Capri, I suppose?

LEO. Hillman Imp.

> **GLORIA** *takes a self-portrait.*

GLORIA. Of course, I prefer Polaroids.

LEO. You need wheels in this life.

GLORIA. Instant gratification.

LEO. Well, I say wheels, I'm still saving up for the tyres.

GLORIA. Like Angel Delight.

RAE. And all to get girls in the back.

LEO. I've not tried, it's on bricks.

RAE. Well, that's fine cos I'm celibate, anyway.

LEO. Celibate?

RAE. A freely-chosen state of sexual abstinence.

GLORIA. Cheekbones.

> **GLORIA** *takes another self-portrait.*

LEO. Like nuns?

RAE. Like artists.

GLORIA. Some artists.

LEO. But why would they do that?

RAE. Sex is an energy, a creative energy. But if you transform it…

GLORIA. Channel it.

RAE. Imagine what art could be then?

LEO. Kinky.

RAE. It's called sexual sublimation. You sublimate desire into friendship or work or creativity.

LEO. Why?

RAE. Because that's what famous artists do, isn't it?

LEO. Like...

RAE. Oh, you know...

GLORIA. Tony Hart.

LEO. Van Goff?

RAE. Van Go'.

GLORIA. There's your exhibition. Voila!

    GLORIA *gives* RAE *the camera and drifts back to the bar.*

LEO. Is that why he cut off his ear?

RAE. He was tortured.

LEO. Who by?

RAE. His innermost thoughts. And sometimes, I know how he felt.

LEO. But your ears are nice.

RAE. Is everything "nice" in your world?

LEO. Tis when I'm with a nice girl.

RAE. I'm not.

LEO. They look good on you, one on each side.

    LEO *flicks* RAE*'s ears.*

RAE. You're invading my space.

LEO. FA Cup, Bristol City!

    LEO *pretends to pick her up by her ears.*

RAE. That hurts!

    LEO *lets go.*

LEO. The last time they got there was 1909. But you don't wanna know that, do you?

    Beat.

RAE. I'm sorry.

LEO. S'alright. I can play with my own.

    LEO *flicks his ears.*

RAE. Leo?

As **LEO** *looks up,* **RAE** *takes his photograph.*

LEO. Mugshot.

RAE. Portrait.

LEO. Yeh.

RAE. Nice.

> **LEO** *flicks his ears again.* **RAE** *takes a picture.*

14.

> PRESSURE DROP *continues as* **RITA** *straightens her clothes.*
> *She tries a few dance steps.* **SAMMY** *shadow-dances with* **RITA.** *He*
> *doesn't touch her. When* **CURTIS** *enters,* **SAMMY** *steps back.*

RITA. How's it looking?

CURTIS. All clear.

RITA. I was starting to think you'd –

CURTIS. I would not leave you.

RITA. I thought perhaps the Military Police –

CURTIS. May I have a moment?

> **CURTIS** *turns from* **RITA** *and comes face-to-face with*
>
> **SAMMY,** *who raises an open palm.* **CURTIS** *punches it hard.*

RITA. It's true what they say about Yanks. You're just like you are in
the films.

CURTIS. You seen *Gone With The Wind?*

RITA. Three times. Clark Gable...

CURTIS. And the smilin' slaves.

RITA. No, I mean, you remind me of him. Almost everything about
you, it's just like you've stepped off the screen.

CURTIS. As what? Servant or idiot boy?

RITA. Your voice. Your accent, your manners, your –

CURTIS. Oh, I ain't no Rhett Butler.

> *Beat.*

RITA. Private?

CURTIS. I went out. All clear. Walked down to Park Street, there's
blood on the sidewalk. My blood.

RITA. How?

CURTIS. I should have stayed out there and fought. For my unit, my country, my race.

RITA. In a street brawl?

CURTIS. We fight fascists wherever they are.

RITA. American fascists? There in't no such thing.

CURTIS. Rita, my grandmother was born a slave. She said "Go to Europe. Stop em out there, you might stop em here".

RITA. But when you get home, things'll change. They will.

CURTIS. How can you possibly know?

RITA. Cos all this… it can't be for nothing.

> **RITA** *takes* **CURTIS** *by the hand.*

CURTIS. How old are you?

RITA. Nineteen.

CURTIS. Twenty-one.

RITA. Say that again.

CURTIS. Twenty-one, ma'am.

RITA. It's Rita. Ma'am makes me sound like the Queen.

CURTIS. Rita.

RITA. I like how you say that, too.

CURTIS. Rita, Rita, Rita.

RITA. Curtis, Curtis, Curtis.

CURTIS. Rita.

RITA. Curtis.

CURTIS. Rita, Rita.

RITA. Curtis, Curtis.

CURTIS. Reeeda!

RITA. Cuuurtis!

CURTIS. *(Bristolian)* Rita.

RITA. *(American)* Wanna know how we dance here, Curtis?

CURTIS. Yes, ma'am.

> **SAMMY** *watches* **RITA** *and* **CURTIS** *waltz into the shadows.*

> *Music cross-fades into* REBEL MUSIC *by Bob Marley.*

15.

GLORIA *swipes a pint from a distracted* YOUNG CLUBBER *and offers it to* SAMMY.

GLORIA. Happy Birthday.

SAMMY. It's not.

GLORIA. Have it anyway.

SAMMY. Piss off.

GLORIA. Have it thrown in your face?

SAMMY. Like you would. Jesus…

SAMMY *takes the pint.*

GLORIA. I wanna talk to you, that's all.

SAMMY. Yeh? Tough.

GLORIA. Man-to-man.

SAMMY. You're full of it.

GLORIA. Full to the brim, just like you.

SAMMY. I'm nothing like you.

GLORIA. Still waters run deep.

SAMMY. Stormy waters.

GLORIA. Poetic.

SAMMY. You want a poem? "There was an old queer from St. Paul's" –

GLORIA. You know me so well.

SAMMY. I know you're bent as a tap.

GLORIA. So? There's more things in heaven and earth, Horatio.

SAMMY. Horatio?

GLORIA. Hamlet.

SAMMY. Ain't that a cigar?

Beat.

GLORIA. That's funny. You're funny.

SAMMY. You are. In the head.

GLORIA. But you're all right? After being away like you was?

SAMMY. Course I am.

GLORIA. Cos I know what them places –

SAMMY. I am.

SAMMY *crosses the club.*

Music cross-fades to ROOMING HOUSE BOOGIE.

SAMMY *sees* **CURTIS** *and* **RITA** *dance out of the shadows.*

RITA. Won't you be missed at the base?

CURTIS. They can flog me til dawn for all I care.

RITA. I told Father I'd be home for eleven. He waits up, he worries.

CURTIS. I'll walk ya.

RITA. But not just yet.

CURTIS. How about never?

RITA. How long have we been down here, do you think?

CURTIS. Long enough. But not long enough.

RITA. See? You're a poet.

CURTIS. But you know what I'm saying?

RITA. I think so. Of course.

CURTIS. So shall we stop talking and –

> **CURTIS** *goes to kiss* **RITA**. *She pulls back.*

RITA. No.

> **SAMMY** *is watching.*

CURTIS. Pardon me.

RITA. It's all right.

CURTIS. I thought you were…

RITA. I was. It ain't you. I'm… engaged.

CURTIS. You are?

RITA. He's away, my fiancé. Far East. It's three years since I saw him. I can't wear a ring with the work I do, see?

CURTIS. Oh, sure.

RITA. So that's why… it ain't cos… it's that.

> *Beat.*

CURTIS. Then I'll walk you home.

RITA. Thank you.

CURTIS. Make sure you're safe.

RITA. I'm sure I will be, with you.

> *Beat.*

CURTIS. Rita…

RITA. Curtis.

CURTIS. Should we blow out the candles?

RITA. Yes.

> **CURTIS** *and* **RITA** *each blow out a candle.* **RITA** *kisses* **CURTIS.** *They move into the shadows. As they go,* **SASHA** *comes out of the toilets.*

SASHA. Enough! Enough, enough, enough, enough, enough!

> *Music cross-fades to* RETURN OF DJANGO *by The Upsetters.*

16.

> **SASHA** *runs to the payphone.* **SAMMY** *goes to follow her but* **HOLLY** *cuts in.* **LEO** *is behind the bar, where* **RAE** *takes his photo.*

LEO. *(DA)* Know what? This isn't a good job. Nah, it's the best bloody job in the world! There may be all sorts of trouble out there but down here, with the girls and booze and the music... where else in the world would you be?

> **HOLLY** *reaches* **SASHA,** *who has picked up the phone.*

HOLLY. What's going on?

SASHA. What do you care?

HOLLY. Sasha?

SASHA. I've been in the toilets for ten whole minutes and nobody – nobody – came.

HOLLY. Who are you phoning?

SASHA. A taxi.

HOLLY. To go where?

> **SASHA** *is dialing a number.*

SASHA. I don't care. Anywhere. Weston.

HOLLY. Weston?

SASHA. If they ever pick up.

HOLLY. Sod Weston, let's take it to London.

SASHA. With three pounds in my purse?

HOLLY. So? We'll jump out and run. They won't expect girls to do that.

> *Beat.*

SASHA. We can't.

HOLLY. No? We could have been murdered last night.

SASHA. Yes, I know but –

HOLLY. So we can do anything, can't we? There's nothing to fear. We can go where we like. Go to London, get jobs and get sorted.

SASHA. London…

HOLLY. Put all this behind us, all right? Done.

> HOLLY *takes the receiver and puts it down.*

SASHA. It isn't as simple as that.

HOLLY. 'Tis to me. There's places in London. We'll sort it.

SASHA. Will we?

HOLLY. I swear.

> *Beat.*

SASHA. I'm sorry.

HOLLY. What for?

SASHA. Dragging you into all this.

HOLLY. You didn't. I'm here cos I wanna be, Sash.

> HOLLY *kisses* SASHA *on the lips.*

SASHA. Holly, you can't do that here.

HOLLY. Do what?

SASHA. Sammy's watching. He might get the wrong –

> SAMMY *moves towards them.* GLORIA *is watching.*

HOLLY. He made a pass at me, Sasha.

SASHA. He what?

HOLLY. He wanted to go to the Downs. Tonight. He couldn't care less about you.

SASHA. Christ…

HOLLY. But I do.

GLORIA. Well, well…

HOLLY. I do.

> HOLLY *kisses* SASHA *again.*

> SAMMY *stops.*

SASHA. Actually, no!

HOLLY. What's the matter?

SASHA. I've told you, I'm straight.

HOLLY. You go with black boys.

SASHA. There's a subtle difference.

HOLLY. There wasn't last night.

SASHA. Last night? Nothing happened.

HOLLY. You think so?

SASHA. I know.

HOLLY. We slept in your bed.

SASHA. Yes, we slept.

HOLLY. But the feeling was –

SASHA. Holly, we slept.

     SASHA *runs downstairs, passing* **SAMMY**.

SAMMY. Sasha?

SASHA. No!

     GLORIA *goes to* **HOLLY** *as she shouts after* **SASHA**.

HOLLY. You want to run? I'll give you something to run from.

GLORIA. So what do you do for an encore?

HOLLY. You'll see.

GLORIA. She's not that kind of girl, you know that?

HOLLY. She's an artist, ain't she? Well, she made out she was.

GLORIA. When?

HOLLY. After the bomb. I found my way to a phone box, didn't know who else to call. We got drunk on her mum's home-made wine. She talked about art and then him. Said "Do you know what it's like, loving someone you won't ever have?"

GLORIA. Love, how sixties.

HOLLY. I told her: "I do, as it happens." And said how I felt.

GLORIA. About her?

HOLLY. Except I don't any more.

     GLORIA *is watching* **HOLLY** *making a new call.*

GLORIA. So what now? You'll scream or you'll die or go stark raving mad on the dance floor?

HOLLY. No. Better than that.

GLORIA. We should all lose our minds. As soon as we can, it's the future.

HOLLY. I'll show you the future.

GLORIA. 999?

HOLLY. I'll show them all.

GLORIA. You're reporting her? What for?

> **HOLLY** *speaks in an Irish accent.*

HOLLY. Listen up, yeh. There's a bomb by The Dug Out on Park Row. The Dug Out, that's right. We've come back to finish the job.

> **HOLLY** *bangs the receiver down.*

GLORIA. You didn't?

HOLLY. I did.

GLORIA. So it really is 'make war not love' now?

HOLLY. It's art.

> *Music cross-fades back to* ROOMING HOUSE BOOGIE.

> **CURTIS** *and* **RITA** *partner each other. The* **YOUNG CLUBBERS** *dance together.* **SAMMY, SASHA, LEO, RAE, GLORIA** *and* **HOLLY** *messily swap partners. All the joy and confusion of the night is captured in the dance.*

> *At the climactic moment, the dance is shattered by the combined noise of two major incidents in the street: boots on the tarmac, soldiers shouts and threats, bottles thrown and broken; 1970s police sirens, a police megaphone warning, people running and shouting, car doors slamming and metal dustbins upturned.*

ACT TWO

1.

Later that night. The lights are on. **LEO** *tunes* **SAMMY**'s *radio to the police shortwave. The clubbers listen to the ghostly signals from the operation.*

LEO. *(TA)* The cops came in. Turned on the lights, cut the music, put us on lock-down. They're searching in dustbins on Park Row. The girls are upset but I've told 'em, if something goes off, we're better down here. And it isn't a bomb that'll kill us, it's boredom.

SAMMY. What are you doing with that?

LEO. Police shortwave. Top of the AM dial. We'd we'd tune as kids, remember?

SAMMY. No.

SAMMY takes the radio.

RAE. What are they saying?

LEO. They've not found nothing yet.

SASHA hears the word 'Clifton' on the shortwave.

SASHA. They're searching in Clifton?

LEO. Nah, that's a cabbie.

SAMMY retunes the radio. A local pirate reggae station plays HOUSEWIVES CHOICE *by Derrick & Patsy.*

RAE. They can't keep us locked up like this.

LEO. Locked down, it's different. And they can do what they want til it's safe.

HOLLY. Who wants to be safe?

LEO. Ah, the micks'll be long gone by now. If it was them in the first place.

GLORIA. Really? Do you think it's a hoax?

40

HOLLY. Who'd do something like that?

LEO. Some Nailsea mong. They'd have shipped us all out if it weren't.

GLORIA. What'd happen to them if they're caught?

HOLLY. They won't be. You can't trace a ten-second call.

GLORIA. But we don't know it was ten seconds, do we?

LEO. Ah, whatever it was, they're not gonna get us tonight.

HOLLY. Unless it's in here?

RAE. What?

HOLLY. The bomb. In the cloakroom, the toilets –

SASHA. Don't be ridiculous.

HOLLY. Them other places –

RAE. Birmingham, Guildford.

HOLLY. They were in pubs.

RAE. So why aren't they searching, why haven't they looked, why –

LEO. There's no IRA nothing in here, right?

RAE. How do you know?

LEO. But there's enough booze to blow off the roof. On the house, I say, tonight. Drinking game!

RAE. That's hardly appropriate, given –

LEO. Never Have I Ever, you know it?

> **LEO** *goes to the bar for bottles of spirits.*

HOLLY. I do. I say something I've never done –

GLORIA. Like planted a bomb.

HOLLY. And if *you've* done it, you get a shot.

GLORIA. Bang!

LEO. Simple as Snap, innit? Go on then, sort yourselves out.

> **SAMMY** *corners* **LEO**.

SAMMY. Leo? Where's the back door?

LEO. There in't one.

SAMMY. You sure?

LEO. Cool your boots, man. We'll be out soon enough.

SAMMY. Cool your boots? I've been banged up for six weeks.

LEO. Just stay where you are.

SAMMY. No chance.

SAMMY *goes to exit but* **LEO** *pulls him back.*

LEO. Sammy! There's too many coppers.

SAMMY. I'll have 'em.

LEO. Sit down. Sit!

> **LEO** *pushes* **SAMMY** *back into the club. The jolt retunes the radio to* I LEARNED ABOUT LOVE FROM HER *by Cab Calloway.*

2.

> **CURTIS** *emerges from the shadows, half-dressed.* **RITA** *watches as he finds his cigarette case.*
>
> **CURTIS** *lights the cigarette and offers it to* **RITA.**
>
> **SAMMY** *takes his notebook from his pocket.*

CURTIS. So, what does an Air Force girl do?

RITA. Seems you know very well.

CURTIS. At work. Clean and such?

RITA. It ain't very interesting.

CURTIS. You're very interesting. What?

RITA. Well, at first, yes we cleaned.

CURTIS. The officers latrines, their beds?

RITA. Well, no. But there was plenty of polishing: cutlery, buttons, every spare minute, we're shining our shoes. Then after all that, it's drill.

CURTIS. You drill?

RITA. We gave it a try. I like to dance so I picked it up but the others, oh my! Some were so bad, they had their own squad.

CURTIS. That I would like to see.

RITA. Still, we passed out in the end. Then you're in with the air crew, the engineers, the technicians.

CURTIS. It's operational?

RITA. I'll say. You know you're at war then, I tell you.

CURTIS. And you're there thinking "Man, what I'd do if I could".

RITA. Well, yes, I suppose we all want to do more.

CURTIS. I was posted to Fort Logan, Colorado. We're there to be trained in armed combat. Instead we're digging ditches, washing dishes, waiting tables. A pal of mine, he asks to go to tyre maintenance school but 'no coloureds with whites'.

RITA. Even in class?

CURTIS. Mealtimes, we're stood outside mess til the white troops are done.

RITA. To eat what's left?

CURTIS. You know, I don't wanna be talking like this.

RITA. I don't mind.

CURTIS. Well, I do. Pardon me, ma'am.

RITA. Ma'am?

CURTIS. So where have they put'cha at Pucklechurch? Kitchen or stores? Or are you still cleaning the base?

RITA. Oh, I just operate barrage balloons.

CURTIS. Operate?

RITA. Yes, splice the winch, drive the wire. It's not hard once you know how. Hands like leather, look.

CURTIS. Calf-skin. Go on.

RITA. But I started… back when… as an R/T Operator.

CURTIS. R/T?

RITA. Radio Telephone. In the Watch Office. Talking down the aircrews when they come back from ops.

CURTIS. Girls do that here?

RITA. I was only picked cos I've got a clear voice.

CURTIS. You spoke to the pilots?

RITA. We just followed procedure. It was pretty routine. Set replies and instructions: A for Apple, B for Beer, C for Charles and all that.

CURTIS. And the guys, they accept you?

RITA. They had to admit we brightened things up. We made tea too, that helped. And we weren't what they called Aircraft Comforts.

CURTIS. What's that?

RITA. We didn't join up just to get us a man. You see, all this, it isn't my usual…

CURTIS. I know that.

RITA. Oh. Does it show?

CURTIS. No.

RITA. I mean, really, it isn't… You're first in line, Curtis, this time.

> **SAMMY** *tunes the radio back to **HOUSEWIVES CHOICE** and puts his notebook in his pocket.*

3.

> **LEO, RAE, HOLLY, SASHA** *and* **GLORIA** *are sat in a circle. They are drinking shots. The bottles are spread around them.*

LEO. Never have I ever peed in a swimming pool.

HOLLY. If you have, then you drink.

LEO. Or swim with your trap shut.

> **SAMMY** *circles the game with a bottle in his hand.*

HOLLY. Sasha?

SASHA. Never have I ever… broken a bone.

GLORIA. How boring.

SASHA. I'm not! Am I?

> **RAE, HOLLY** *and* **SAMMY** *drink.*

HOLLY. Raymond?

RAE. Rae. Never have I ever had sex with a man. I'm quite open about it.

> **HOLLY, SASHA** *and* **GLORIA** *drink.*

GLORIA. Never have I ever been 'open'.

LEO. Well, I have, I can't help myself. Cheers!

> **LEO** *drinks.*

HOLLY. Never have I ever made a girl kiss me.

LEO. All right, yeh, I think once I have.

> **LEO** *drinks.*

HOLLY. But she liked it?

LEO. Oh, definitely.

RAE. Excuse me, do you know what that was?

LEO. Just a kiss.

HOLLY. 'Just' a kiss? No such thing.

SASHA. Course there is.

HOLLY. No, it always means something.

RAE. Except to men.

LEO. It means something to me, every time.

GLORIA. Well, we'll see. Spin-the-Bottle!

> GLORIA *rolls a bottle to the centre of the circle.*

SASHA. We're playing Never Have I –

GLORIA. Like I said, boring. Spin the bottle. Kiss whoever it points to when it stops. Boy, girl or boy/girl, if you dare.

SAMMY. *(to GLORIA)* What are you doing here, ey?

GLORIA. Conversation at last.

LEO. Sammy...

SAMMY. There's places for bum-boys like you.

GLORIA. Oh, I know that. In side streets with unmarked back doors.

LEO. Never Have I Ever –

GLORIA. But when I go, the peep-hole slams shut. *(camp)* "Sorry, dear. It's men only in here".

SAMMY. Well, why don't you look like you're meant to, then? Kevin.

> *Silence.*

GLORIA. Kevin?

SAMMY. That's your real name, ain't it?

RAE. *(amused)* Kevin?

SASHA. Rae...

SAMMY. And you work for the Post Office.

GLORIA. Never have I ever grown so bored of a game.

LEO. Me too, shall we just drink?

RAE. *(laughing)* Kevin!

HOLLY. Know what? We should go up and kick down that door.

SASHA. *(laughing too)* Stop it!

HOLLY. We should kick it in now. Get out of the nursery.

RAE. What nursery?

HOLLY. This one. Full of posh girls who'll never grow up.

RAE. Oh, really?

LEO. Rae, don't make it no worse than it –

HOLLY. Art school? Play School.

> RAE *throws a pint over* HOLLY.

LEO. Blimey, Rae.

> **HOLLY** *turns and takes a slow walk to the Ladies.*

RAE. Who's turn is it?

GLORIA. Leo? Lost Property box, please.

LEO. Why?

GLORIA. We've got a new game. It's called Go to Hell.

> **LEO** *takes the box from behind the bar and gives it to* **GLORIA.**

> **YOUNG CLUBBER 1** *has passed out on the floor with a bottle of rum in his hand.* **GLORIA** *takes the rum and the box and follows* **HOLLY** *into the Ladies.*

4.

> *The radio plays* THE WHOLE WORLD'S DOWN ON ME *by Ken Boothe. A few* **YOUNG CLUBBERS** *idly dance but most lie around drinking and waiting.*

LEO. *(TA)* Tick-tock-tick-tock-tick-tock-tick. One more hour you'll never get back. One more night passes and nothing has changed. The future is now, man, it's now, man, it's now. And what are you doing with it, ey?

SAMMY. Leo?

> **SAMMY** *holds out his glass for a refill.*

LEO. Shit-head.

SAMMY. You knew him at school.

LEO. I knew you, an' all. But that was a lifetime ago.

> **RAE** *raises her glass.*

RAE. To the end of exams.

SASHA. To the summer. Can't come soon enough.

RAE. To art school.

> *Beat.*

SASHA. Yes.

RAE. To our last night on earth, who knows?

LEO. If it does end tonight, I've had a good life.

RAE. You're seventeen.

LEO. That's what I'm saying. I'll die young and handsome.

RAE. With no regrets?

LEO. Nah, not my thing.

RAE. Well, it should be. A life unexamined, and all that.

LEO. All what?

RAE. 'A life unexamined is not worth living'.

LEO. Who said that, then?

>   *Beat.*

RAE. I forget but it's famous.

LEO. Weren't Socrates, then?

SASHA. It might have been, yes.

LEO. Encyclopedia Brittanica.

RAE. Oh.

LEO. The door-to-door salesman came round. Mur signed up, so I thought I'd show willing. That's how I learnt about engines, you see? Internal combustion, two-stroke, four stroke, know what that is?

RAE. No.

LEO. Intake, compression, power, and exhaust.

RAE. Marx says man is enslaved by machines.

>   *Beat.*

LEO. I'm doing my best here.

RAE. What do you mean?

LEO. Rae, I just want that smile again.

RAE. I don't do it to order. And perhaps I'm depressed?

LEO. 'Bout what?

RAE. Life.

LEO. Life's what you make it.

RAE. That's such a cliché.

LEO. No, it in't. You want something, you go out and get it, job done.

RAE. So class, race, gender and terrible mothers mean nothing?

SASHA. Rae…

LEO. I can't be doing with all that. Them 'social' things in't stopping me.

RAE. That's what you think.

LEO. They're not. I've got plans, me. Big plans.

RAE. Going into politics, are you?

LEO. No, smart-arse… the Army.

SAMMY. The what?

RAE. Very funny.

LEO. I mean it, I am.

> *Beat.*

RAE. The British Army?

LEO. Course, yeh, what else?

SASHA. Are you sure you don't mean the T.A?

LEO. N.O. I'm gonna sign up next week.

RAE. Why?

LEO. Cos it sorts it all out. The 'What Do You Do' thing, it gives you a future.

RAE. Or takes it away.

LEO. You can go round the world, can't you? Germany, places like that.

RAE. Ireland.

LEO. Well, it can't be no worse than round here. And I handled it, didn't I? Last night, I didn't run.

RAE. What do you mean?

LEO. I was coming up Park Street to work. There were coppers all over, I thought "best not walk through all that and then – wham!" Everything went to slow-motion. A young bloke comes past me with blood on his face. I sat him down in a doorway. Stayed til the ambulance came.

SASHA. Weren't you scared?

LEO. I was shitting it, yeh. But do you know what I found among all the smashed glass? A bottle of milk on a step. As I drank it, I thought 'That's me, Lucky Leo. Still the full pint, see?'

> **LEO** *takes a flattened milk bottle-top from his pocket.*

RAE. The bottle-top.

LEO. Keep me safe, won't it, ey?

RAE. But Leo, you can't.

> *The radio plays* WHAT ABOUT YOU *by Pat Rhoden.*

LEO. I wanna be a mechanic. And the Army, they train you, they properly train you. I could be working on tanks.

RAE. And going to war.

LEO. Ah, there won't be no wars with the nuclear thing. Not old-fashioned ones, anyway.

RAE. But Leo, you're black.

LEO. I'm what? Shit, why weren't I told?

RAE. And you hear about terrible things.

LEO. Like what?

RAE. Like them shoving your head down the toilet and calling you…

LEO. Nig-nog and coon? Well, that's never happened before.

SAMMY *is watching* **LEO.**

RAE. But what does your Mum say? Your Dad?

LEO. My Dad…

RAE. Surely he'll stop you?

LEO. He can't. He's not with us no more.

RAE. Nor is mine, so actually I do understand –

LEO. He died twelve years ago.

RAE. Oh.

LEO. Thirteen next month, weren't it, Sam?

SAMMY. Yeh.

LEO. He served in the Jamaican Defence Force. After the Second World War. So he just might be proud of me, ey?

LEO *glances at* **SAMMY**.

RAE. Well, all right, join them if you must.

LEO. Er, they don't have a regiment here.

RAE. You'd be safer, at least.

LEO. Til Barbados takes over the world, ey?

RAE. You can't go to Belfast. You can't.

LEO. And who are you telling me that? You with your London art school.

RAE. That's totally different.

LEO. Dead right it is. Cos you won't change the world by thinking and talking and taking a picture of it.

RAE. I disagree –

LEO. Course you do but it's my turn, shut up. No, you'll change it by living your life. And I'm not political Rae, not at all. But a black British squaddie, to me, that's…well, there must be a word for it, ey?

SAMMY. Judas.

LEO. You what?

SAMMY. You heard.

RAE. Sammy…

LEO. Say it again!

SAMMY. Oi!

LEO. Say it again, borstal boy.

RAE. Leo?

LEO. Go take some snapshots, ey?

SASHA. *(to* **SAMMY***)* What did he call you?

SAMMY. He's pissed. Thick and pissed.

SASHA. Borstal?

5.

> **LEO** *returns to the bar. As he goes, he turns to the audience.*

LEO. *(DA)* What? Don't look at me for an answer. I'm done here. I've said enough.

> **GLORIA** *comes out of the Ladies and makes a bee-line for* **YOUNG CLUBBER 1**, *who is still unconscious.* **GLORIA** *starts to undo his trousers.*

RAE. What are you doing?

GLORIA. Just a little debagging.

RAE. De-what?

GLORIA. Don't look like that, it's his trousers I want.

RAE. Why?

GLORIA. Shut up and hold this.

> **GLORIA** *gives* **YOUNG CLUBBER 1** *'s leg to* **RAE**.

RAE. Gloria? That wasn't me who… well, not the true me… I was a little bit drunk and –

GLORIA. I know.

GLORIA *pulls off his trousers.*

RAE. I'm a Marxist, you see. I don't look down on anyone.

GLORIA. Oh? I'm a Martian. I do.

> **GLORIA** *goes into the Ladies with the trousers.* **RAE** *lowers* **YOUNG CLUBBER 1** *back to the floor. She looks at him and takes a picture.*

LEO. Rae?

RAE. I'm working.

LEO. I just wanna word with you.

RAE. I'm... no.

> **SAMMY** *and* **SASHA** *share a bottle of vodka.*

SASHA. Where did you go?

SAMMY. Pucklechurch.

SASHA. And what was it like? They treated you fairly, you weren't... singled out?

SAMMY. I didn't get bummed in the shower block, no.

SASHA. Why didn't you write? My father's a barrister, he'd have stepped in –

SAMMY. I take care of myself.

SASHA. I'd have come. If I'd have known, I'd have come.

SAMMY. I know you would. That's why I kept my mouth shut.

> *Beat.*

SASHA. I see.

SAMMY. Not your world, is it?

SASHA. Maybe not but you are.

SAMMY. Piss off.

SASHA. You are.

SAMMY. Is that why you're messing with her?

SASHA. Me? What about you?

SAMMY. I'm not going near her, she's mental.

SASHA. Truly?

SAMMY. She threw herself at me. I know I'm good-looking but shit...

SASHA. And I did it – I danced – to get you to see me. To... I don't know... God, Pucklechurch?

SAMMY. I thought you'd figure it out.

SASHA. How?

SAMMY. I'm here then I'm not. Where else would I be?

SASHA. With a girl.

SAMMY. In't borstal the first thing you think of?

SASHA. Well, actually, no.

Beat.

SAMMY. I just thought you'd figure it out.

Beat.

SASHA. So... six weeks...

SAMMY. On remand.

SASHA. But you're free now, aren't you?

SAMMY. Yeh, free...

SASHA. Yes.

SAMMY. Except sometimes, you're better inside.

SASHA. How can you be?

SAMMY. Thinking 'bout how much you'll change, what you'll say, what you'll do when you're finally... as if the fresh air's gonna fix it.

Beat.

SASHA. Why were you there, Sam? I mean what did you do?

SAMMY. I didn't.

SASHA. What did they say that you did?

SAMMY. Breaking and entering. But I weren't. I were just...where I shouldn't have been. A bloke saw me go over a wall... into one of them gardens than run down the back of your house.

SASHA. You were in Clifton?

SAMMY. Yeh. Looking for you.

SASHA. Sam...

SAMMY. I knew where you lived from walking you home. You said once your room's on the back. And I thought if I got round, chucked a stone at the window, you'd come.

SASHA. Why didn't you just knock on the door?

SAMMY. At midnight? Course, then, the pigs turn up. Corner me. Turns out there's been break-ins.

SASHA. There were.

SAMMY. And they found me with forty-five quid. Was fifty but I'd gone and blown five in the pub.

SASHA. What were you doing with all that?

SAMMY. What do you think?

SASHA. Right…

SAMMY. I don't know how much it costs but I got what I could.

SASHA. How?

SAMMY. Don't matter now.

SASHA. It does to me. How?

Beat.

SAMMY. I took a few parcels from St. Paul's to Clifton.

SASHA. What kind of parcels?

SAMMY. For the hippies, you know?

SASHA. Christ, if they'd caught you –

SAMMY. They didn't.

SASHA. You could have got years.

SAMMY. I know what I'm doing.

SASHA. Oh? Is it a regular thing?

SAMMY. Do I look like it is? But it's there if I need it and that night I did.

SASHA. You mean I did?

SAMMY. Not your fault, is it? None of it.

SASHA. So how come you're angry with me?

SAMMY. I'm angry with everything, aren't I?

Beat.

SASHA. What was it like in there? What did you do with yourself?

SAMMY. Ah, I just sat on my arse for the first week and thought about things…

SASHA. What things?

SAMMY. This and that.

SASHA. You and me?

SAMMY. Everything. Then I thought about nothing at all. Whole days would go in a… That's how they want you, I suppose. But I thought, 'if I stay here'…the here in my head… 'I might never get back'. So one morning, I went to the workshop. Lads painting toy soldiers with Humbrol, you know? Napolean red,

white and blue. I went just for something to do. Then I started
to think what you say about art, 'bout expressing yourself, an'
all that. So I go to the library. Find a book, *Bristol at War*. Most
of it's boring, to tell you the truth. Except there's a photo. A
black man 'bout my age in a uniform.

Enter **CURTIS** *and* **RITA**, *in uniform. The introduction to*
HARLEM HOSPITALITY *fades up.*

SASHA. Right...

SAMMY. The GI's were in Bristol. Black and white squaddies.
Segregated.

SASHA. From us?

SAMMY. From each other. Jim Crow. Black Tuesday, White
Wednesday, all that.

SASHA. But they're on the same side?

SAMMY. They're fighting each other. Out on Park Street, in the
end. Four hundred American troops in a riot.

SASHA. Out there?

SAMMY. One black GI gets shot dead. And back then, Pucklechurch,
it was an RAF base and I thought to myself... well, I thought
I'd read up on that, too: the airmen, the WAAFS, do you know
what they are?

SASHA. No?

SAMMY. The Women's Auxiliary Air Force, you should do. And
then it came into my head. Two people.

RITA. One black.

CURTIS. One white.

SAMMY. In the war. Wasn't that long ago when you think...and I
started to write.

SASHA. Write?

SAMMY. Yeh. I wrote it down. Every –

CURTIS. Last –

RITA. Word.

SASHA. Wow...

> **SAMMY** *takes out his notebook.*

SAMMY. Don't tell Leo, he'll think I've gone queer.

SASHA. Can I see?

SAMMY. No.

SASHA. Why?

SAMMY. Cos it's bollocks, in'it?

SASHA. All right, tell me. Tell me the story.

 SAMMY *looks to* **CURTIS** *and* **RITA.**

SAMMY. It starts with the riot. A WAAF and a GI, they hide out down here on Park Row. A cellar. Their own dug-out, see? He's thrown a brick and it's hit her. Didn't mean to cause her no harm but she's hurt and he's trying to help…and what they were up against, makes what we're dealing with… I dunno…

SASHA. What happens next?

 Fade up YOU WON'T LET ME GO *by Buddy Johnson.*

6.

 SAMMY *and* **SASHA** *watch* **RITA** *and* **CURTIS.**

RITA. My father…

CURTIS. Let's walk the long way.

RITA. But shouldn't you get back? When they find out you're not at the base…

CURTIS. S'alright, I won't come to the doorstep. I'll stay at the end of the street.

RITA. No, no… father likes your… He says you're well-mannered, more so than the whites.

CURTIS. He just don't want 'em dating his girl.

RITA. Dating?

CURTIS. It's okay, I know… your fiancé. But couldn't we go to the movies? Meet for 'a nice cup of tea'. Go someplace and just talk.

RITA. There is no fiancé. Not in the Far East or anywhere else. And there won't be, I'm sorry. Not til the end of the war.

CURTIS. Why?

RITA. Because I'll be at Pucklechurch, you'll be in France –

CURTIS. Or still driving trucks on the base.

RITA. Either way, we can't have… close attachments.

CURTIS. Says who?

 Beat.

RITA. I won't see you again, will I?

CURTIS. Well, if that's what you want?

Beat.

RITA. There's a reason I'm here. Back in Bristol, I mean. I was transferred from my last post, and perhaps we should go now?

CURTIS. Not yet.

RITA. I took a Darky call nine months ago.

CURTIS. A Darky call?

RITA. The code-word for an aircraft in trouble.

CURTIS. Okay…

RITA. I knew the voice on the line straight away. Frankie, a Scot, 6'2. We'd danced just the night before; he'd walked me back to the barracks and… "Lino-C Charlie calling, may we land"? There's fear in the voice and believe you me, he ain't that sort. We put on the lighting, alert the Crash Crew. "One engine u/s". Over he flies, I call him again: "What else can we do?" Silence. Then "Hello Waddington, I can't…" Call again. No reply. Then the engines come louder than ever. He shoots out of the night to an almighty crash.

CURTIS. Man…

RITA. I look out to a huge ball of fire. We'd lost men before, so many men but all I can think is that mine was the last voice he heard. I was the last girl he'd…and all I remember is somebody's crying and my God, she sounds just like me.

CURTIS. Rita…

RITA. I asked for a transfer. They didn't protest. And I made up my mind that until this war's over… that's it. No more, Curtis. No more.

Beat.

CURTIS. My father was killed by a gang of white men. Beaten to death for refusing to step off the sidewalk when one of 'em wanted to pass.

RITA. In peacetime?

CURTIS *takes* RITA*'s hand.*

CURTIS. Can I please walk you home?

Lights fade on CURTIS *and* RITA.

SASHA. And does he?

SAMMY. Dunno. That's as far as I got.

SASHA. Sammy, you've got to keep going.

SAMMY. Yeh, yeh.

SASHA. And write it up, properly too.

SAMMY. I did it to get me through, that's all. It's done.

SASHA. Have you got a typewriter?

SAMMY. Course not.

SASHA. Mum has, for her poems. You write it, I'll type it. We'll send it to magazines, publishers –

SAMMY. Piss off.

SASHA. You could be a genius, Sam. The James Baldwin of Bristol.

SAMMY. James who?

SASHA. Just think… you can write, I can paint. We'll find a bohemian flat; an attic in Clifton with wonderful light, I've looked in the paper, they don't cost that much. My canvases here, your manuscripts there, a big double bed in the centre. Imagine it, Sammy? Living together, working together, sleeping and waking together.

Beat.

A cot at the end of the bed.

SAMMY. You're having it?

SASHA. I don't know. I just wanted to say it out loud.

SAMMY. Not too loud, ey?

SASHA. It's nearly three months. I'll have to say something soon.

SAMMY. And I want to say this. I'm 21. I've not got a job, I've no chance of a job –

SASHA. You've a talent.

SAMMY. Who says?

SASHA. You're creative and clever and –

SAMMY. You… you're a radical wotsit. A baby don't go with the t-shirt.

SASHA. It might if it's yours. It's almost a statement.

SAMMY. Of what?

SASHA. White woman, black child… the oppressed sort of… coming together.

SAMMY. Hang on? Have you done this deliberate?

SASHA. What do you mean?

SAMMY. To piss off your barrister Dad, to show him how right-on you are.

SASHA. My God, Sam, you're right! "Mum, Dad, you thought I was bourgeois? Well, I go with black boys and I love it."

SAMMY. That's right.

SASHA. I go with you, Sammy. I love you.

SAMMY. Don't tell them that.

SASHA. Are you saying my parents are prejudiced?

SAMMY. Yeh.

SASHA. You've not even met them.

SAMMY. Exactly.

SASHA. I've told Mum about you?

SAMMY. And the half-caste that's coming her way?

> **SASHA** *slaps* **SAMMY** *in the face.*

> **GLORIA** *comes out of the Ladies.*

GLORIA. Stand back, suckers.

> **HOLLY** *follows. She wears a tonic suit jacket,* **YOUNG CLUBBER**
> 1 *'s trousers and a pork pie hat. She looks like a beautiful*
> *androgynous boy.*

LEO. Shit.

RAE. God.

GLORIA. No. Fallen angel.

SASHA. *(to* **SAMMY***)* Go on, then. Finish the job – hit me back.

HOLLY. Oh no, you don't.

SASHA. I'm a pregnant girl. Beat me up, bad man, if that's what you are.

RAE. Pregnant?

> **HOLLY** *swaggers over.*

HOLLY. Yep. All right, Dad?

SAMMY. Piss off, pervert.

RAE. *(to* **LEO***)* She's…

LEO. Ah, shit.

HOLLY. You wanna fight?

SASHA. Holly, stay out of this

HOLLY. Come on, then. Fight!

SAMMY. I don't hit girls.

HOLLY. I'm not a girl.

GLORIA. Frankenstein's monster malfunctions.

HOLLY. I'm everything you are, so fight.

GLORIA. Back to the lab, Holly.

HOLLY. Fight!

GLORIA. Relaxez-vous.

SAMMY. Get out of my face, batty-man.

GLORIA. Would that be your black face, my lover?

> **SAMMY** *turns from* **HOLLY** *and punches* **GLORIA** *in the face.*

HOLLY. No!

SASHA. Christ!

RAE. Get the bouncers, the police!

LEO. No! They'll send him back down.

RAE. Down?

SASHA. Well, that's it. We're over, we're done!

> **HOLLY** *goes to* **GLORIA.**

HOLLY. It's all right, I'm here.

GLORIA. I'm glad one of us is. Help me up.

> **SAMMY** *drags* **LEO** *aside.*

SAMMY. Leo? How much cash have you got?

LEO. What do you mean?

SAMMY. I'm going, what have you got?

LEO. Going where?

SAMMY. What?

LEO. Nothing for you.

SAMMY. Leo –

GLORIA. Oh, Sammy? Before you depart...

> **GLORIA** *pulls* **SAMMY** *to face her.*

SAMMY. Oi!

> **GLORIA** *kisses* **SAMMY** *on the lips.*

GLORIA. With love from Kev.

SAMMY. You dirty –

GLORIA. You're right. And I fight dirty, too.

GLORIA *knees* **SAMMY** *in the groin.*

SASHA. Stop!

GLORIA. You see, Sammy, we're one and the same. I've had to fight every day of my life… and just by existing, I win.

As **GLORIA** *turns,* **SAMMY** *pulls him over by the ankle.*

SAMMY. You reckon?

A vicious fight ensues. **SAMMY** *and* **GLORIA** *punch, kick,) scratch, bite and curse. A second fight breaks out among the* **YOUNG CLUBBERS**. *Finally,* **GLORIA** *pins* **SAMMY** *down and pulls a Stanley knife.*

GLORIA. Reckon with this.

SAMMY. Shit!

GLORIA. Not scared of me, are you?

SAMMY. Put it down.

GLORIA. Oh, come on, you can't be.

HOLLY. Gloria –

GLORIA. Cos I was your best mate on Ashley Road.

LEO. That Kev?

GLORIA. Ten years old. Knock-and-run, nicking sweets, telling all sorts of tales. Our two crazy heads in the clouds.

LEO. But you're not crazy now, are you, ey?

GLORIA. The Bus Boycott. I did that with you.

SAMMY. Yeh, I know.

GLORIA. They wouldn't give jobs to the blacks but I stood up against 'em, with you.

The payphone rings. **YOUNG CLUBBER 2** *goes to answer it.*

YOUNG CLUBBER 2. Hello? *(listens, then holds out the receiver).* Leo? It's your Mur.

LEO. Shit…

YOUNG CLUBBER 2 *hands* **LEO** *the phone and exits.* **GLORIA** *looks at* **SAMMY** *and laughs.*

SAMMY. Kev…

GLORIA. Your Mur.

HOLLY *takes the knife from* **GLORIA**.

LEO. Mur?… Yeh, I know what the time is… I'm still working, aren't I… cashing up, cooling down… well, that's me, conscientious… no, nothing's wrong… nothing's happened, Mur… I swear on the Bible I'm safe… Look, are you in a phonebox?… You shouldn't be out there at night… But you CAN sleep, we're grown now, we're…there's the pips, Mur… you go home to bed, ey? You… She's gone.

LEO *puts the phone down. Outside, a police siren sounds and fades into the distance.* **YOUNG CLUBBER 2** *enters.*

YC. It's all over. We can go home now.

SAMMY *is back on his feet.*

SASHA. Sammy –

SAMMY. No.

SAMMY *retreats.*

The DJ plays KUNG FU FIGHTING *by Carl Douglas.*

The **YOUNG CLUBBERS** *start to leave.*

HOLLY *turns to* **GLORIA.**

HOLLY. Tea and toast by the fire at yours?

GLORIA. Fire? It's a two-bar electric.

HOLLY. My favourite fuel.

GLORIA. But you know what they say: life's a gas.

HOLLY. And I take it there's no-one at home?

GLORIA. Just my fox fur and crocodile shoes.

HOLLY. Good, so there's room in your bed.

GLORIA. If you keep your hands to yourself.

HOLLY. Oh, I will. Cross my heart, hope to die.

GLORIA. Tragically.

HOLLY. With a bottle of gin, a handful of pills and nothing on but Chanel Number 5.

GLORIA. You're staying?

HOLLY. You might have a funny turn in the night.

GLORIA. My dear, I am a funny turn in the night.

HOLLY. Get out.

As **HOLLY** *and* **GLORIA** *go,* **GLORIA** *turns to* **SAMMY**.

GLORIA. See you next week?

SAMMY *nods.*

GLORIA *smiles and leaves with a Sally Bowles wave.*

LEO, RAE, SASHA *and* SAMMY *recover themselves.*

YOUNG CLUBBER 1 *wakes, stands up but doesn't quite know where he is. He looks down at his bare legs and looks back, as if his trousers might be following. He shrugs and stumbles out of the club.*

7.

LEO *is closing the bar. The* YOUNG CLUBBERS *gradually make their way out.* RAE *is at the bar with* SASHA.

LEO. *(TA)* You see now why I wanna sign up? Cos it's a simple life, ain't it? 'Stand up, turn around, walk over there' Do what you're told, think what you're told'. Wish I could. Wish I could...

RAE. Why didn't you tell me?

SASHA. Cos you'd have told Mum.

RAE. I wouldn't.

SASHA. You would. You of all people can't hide things from her.

RAE. How long have you known?

SASHA. Long enough.

RAE. Seen a doctor?

SASHA. Not yet.

RAE. So you might still be wrong?

SASHA. No. You know your own body, don't you?

RAE. I haven't even had sex.

SASHA. Holly thinks I should have an abortion.

RAE. You talked to her first?

SASHA. She's an outsider. That made it easier, somehow.

Beat.

RAE. And she's right. Of course you should. Yes.

LEO. Rae?

RAE. Not now.

LEO. I just wanted to ask… Seeing as we're not, you know, dead or –

RAE. There's nothing to say. You're a soldier, I'm a pacifist.

LEO. You do nothing but fight. And I might have flat feet yet, ey?

LEO does a soft-shoe shuffle.

RAE. I can't…

SASHA. Can't what?

RAE. Cos as soon as I do… as soon as I think, 'Wow, they like what they see' or 'they might understand' or 'they'll stick around'… well, they're men, they don't.

SASHA. How do you know? You've not had one.

RAE. All right, it isn't just men, it's everyone. Except you and your Mum.

SASHA. But we can't be your everything, Rae. You have to let someone else in.

RAE. I don't want to. I'm fine. I just want to be on my own.

LEO. Wanna come see my car, anyway?

Beat.

RAE. When?

LEO. No time like right now. Its like me, it looks good in the dark.

RAE. And what then?

LEO. You can sleep on the sofa. Mur won't mind.

RAE. Won't she?

LEO. A girl in the house? S'what she's been waiting for, innit?

SASHA. Really?

LEO. Not a girlfriend, of course. A friend-girl. Woman.

RAE. Friend-girl…

LEO. Someone to talk to, ain't it? Better than two dumb-head sons.

Beat.

RAE. You're not.

LEO. Well, I do my best, ey? Are you coming or what?

RAE gestures to SASHA.

RAE. I really should…

SASHA. I'll see you tomorrow. For dinner, all right?

RAE. At yours?

SASHA. Don't be late.

RAE. Be careful.

SASHA. It's a bit late for that.

> *Beat.*

You too.

RAE. I'll try.

> **RAE** *hugs* **SASHA** *and exits.*

LEO. *(TA)* Lucky Leo! I'll see you, for sure.

> **LEO** *gives a salute and a wink. He turns to* **SAMMY**.

Sam? I'll see you

> **SAMMY** *nods.*

> **LEO** *follows* **RAE** *out of the club.*

8.

> The Dug Out *falls silent. Only* **SAMMY** *and* **SASHA** *are left.*
> **SAMMY** *watches her preparing to leave.*

SAMMY. Get a taxi.

SASHA. I want to walk.

SAMMY. Safer, innit?

> **SAMMY** *offers* **SASHA** *a pound note.*

SASHA. Is this how we'll live now? Constantly on guard and frightened –

SAMMY. I'm not.

SASHA. You get a taxi. There's police –

SAMMY. I won't belt 'em, if that's what you think.

SASHA. Nor will I.

SAMMY. Good. Once your dukes are up, Jeez…

SASHA. That's the first time I've ever hit someone.

SAMMY. S'alright, didn't hurt. Well, not much.

> *A moment between them.*

SASHA. What?

SAMMY. That night. I shoulda come out prepared.

SASHA. So should I. But you don't think it'll ever…

SAMMY. And the pulling-out thing, that's crap.

SASHA. It might work if you actually did it.

SAMMY. I did. Well, I tried.

SASHA. It's all right. I didn't want you to either.

Beat.

SAMMY. Get yourself on the pill, ey?

SASHA. Good advice, Sammy. Thank you, I will.

SAMMY. Get on the pill and I'll find us a flat. Stand by you, do the right thing.

SASHA. Shotgun wedding?

SAMMY. If that's what you want.

SASHA. You're proposing?

SAMMY. I'm not the black bastard who leaves the white girl.

Beat.

SASHA. I see.

SAMMY. You don't. Why would you? But bring up a black kid, you'll have to.

SASHA. It's not a 'black kid', it's our kid.

SAMMY. And I'm 21 now. I can step into them shoes. I'll get us the money to… somehow, I will.

SASHA *takes a long look at* SAMMY.

SASHA. We can't.

SAMMY. Why not?

SASHA. We haven't begun our own lives, never mind…

SAMMY. You said you wanted it?

SASHA. That's not the same thing as having it. Not in the real world. You know that better than me.

SAMMY. I've seen enough of the real world.

SASHA. That's why you can write, Sam. That's why you have to.

YOU WON'T LET ME GO *by Buddy Johnson quietly plays.*

CURTIS *and* RITA *return to dance.*

SAMMY. Can I… can I please walk you home?

SASHA. Can we talk to my parents together?

SAMMY. And then?

SASHA. I'll see a doctor. Sit my exams. Go to art school. Live my life.

SAMMY. Good.

SASHA. But Sam, if you want to be part of it… and if you want me in yours…?

SAMMY. I'm out. I'm a free man.

SASHA. Let's go.

> **SAMMY** *looks at* **SASHA**.

SAMMY. Not til you've danced with me.

SASHA. Now?

SAMMY. It's The Dug Out.

SASHA. There's no music.

> **SAMMY** *puts his arms around* **SASHA**.

SAMMY. Imagine.

> **SAMMY** *and* **SASHA** *dance.*

> **CURTIS** *and* **RITA** *dance.*

> *Fade to black.*

THE END.

.

Lightning Source UK Ltd.
Milton Keynes UK
UKOW02f1238021214

242517UK00001B/19/P

9 780573 110429